COYOTE TALES
FROM THE INDIAN PUEBLOS

by
Evelyn Dahl Reed

Illustrations By Glen Strock

SUNSTONE
PRESS

SANTA FE
NEW MEXICO

Printed in the United States of America

10 9 8 7 6

Library of Congress Cataloging in Publication Data:
Reed, Evelyn Dahl, 1906-
    Coyote tales from the Indian pueblos.

    Bibliography: p.
    1. Pueblo Indians—Legends. 2. Coyote (Legendary character)
    3. Indians of North America—Southwest.
New—Legends. I. Title.
E99.P9R27   1988   398.2'452974442   86-14544

ISBN: 0-86534-094-3 (pbk.)

Published by SUNSTONE PRESS
           Post Office Box 2321
           Santa Fe, NM 87504-2321 / USA
           (505) 988-4418 / orders only (800) 243-5644
           FAX (505) 988-1025

CONTENTS

THE STORY SOURCES

It is an old academic question whether or not animal stories existed as Indian oral tradition among the Pueblos before Europeans came to the Southwest. Such tales as "The Medicine Man" and "The Thunder Knives" may be indigenous. Others, like "The Pine Gum Baby," told to Elsie Clews Parsons at Santa Clara by a man with an adoptive mother from Taos, and "The Discontented Farmer," told to Charles Lummis in 1891 by gray-haired Felipe, of Isleta, are almost certainly borrowed from the Old World. But all are entertaining in Indian dress, and that is the basis for the stories included here.

In the sequence, ancient and modern tales are intermingled. They could have been separated only at the sacrifice of readability. These tales have been adapted from the literature buried in the nether regions of museums and libraries and from firsthand tellings of men and women in the Pueblos. For the assiduous collecting of many tales, some of which are retold here, we are deeply indebted to Charles Lummis, Father Noel Dumarest, John Gunn, Elsie Parsons, Ruth Benedict, Elizabeth DeHuff, and others.

Sometimes a story may be unknown in one Pueblo and have several popular variants in another. "The Tail Race" is told at Jémez of Coyote and Woodchuck. At Santo Domingo, the Quail play the trick of fastening a topknot on Coyote's head. At Isleta, the music teacher is Locust instead of Horned Toad. At Cochiti, it is the Roadrunner Girls with whom Coyote wants to grind meal. A few stories, such as "The Spotted Deer," seem to be universal. There are eight versions in print: Isleta, (Lummis), San

Juan (Parsons), San Ildefonso (Espinosa), Cochiti (Benedict), Sia (Stevenson), Laguna (Parsons), Hopi (DeHuff), Apache (Opler), while the variant related here was told to me at Jémez.

Properly told, the Pueblo animal story is strictly anecdotal, with a formal opening and ending as given here. Winter is the time for storytelling. And evening is the favorite hour. Children gather around the fire, and some older person tells stories interminably, or until all the young ones have fallen asleep.

In the animal tales of the Pueblos, Coyote is the scapegoat, the meddling, cowardly, proverbially stupid fellow, not to be confused with Fox, who is very wise. Observe the costume details of the ceremonial dancers, and you will see the fox pelt as an exalted symbol in the religious hierarchy. Only the sacred clowns wear the coyote pelt.

Nevertheless, there is a favorite theme in Pueblo lore that no one is so homely or so dull as not to have some gift for the good of others. Hence, Coyote's misadventures are instructive for the young. These tales, though told for hundreds of years, have a vigor and beauty that only brightens with retelling for children everywhere.

Evelyn Reed

COYOTE — THE ENDURING SYMBOL

One of the most constant symbols of North American Indian mythology is Coyote, a figure that has not only persisted but successfully crossed cultural barriers. Coyote survives both as an animal and a myth in literature and art. Contemporary artists such as Harry Fonseca have made a cult of the coyote figure and perpetuated the various legends associated with him.

Coyote is a dichotomous figure. He is perceived as a trickster, a helper, teacher, a fool and a creator. In other words, he is both good and evil. It is said that he possesses every quality of mankind and like humans, he is sometimes a villain, sometimes victim; sometimes a predator, sometimes a savior. And, also like mankind, Coyote is resourceful, tough and enduring.

The trickster is a common character in folktales and Coyote is the best known of the Indian trickster figures. Often depicted as licentious, greedy and a braggart, Coyote is sometimes accompanied by an animal friend. This companion may serve as a foil or an unwitting victim of Coyote's tricks.

Coyote is also a hero figure and creator, a demi-god not unlike the Greek Gods in whom were combined divine attributes and human lust and greed. In some myths, Coyote is the one who got fire and daylight for man and taught him how to be a hunter. Coyote is also thought to have curative powers. According to Crow Indian mythology, the Sun-Coyote created the earth and made living creatures for it.

In some legends, Coyote becomes the one being tricked or the scapegoat. He is frequently bested by those who exploit his greed or turn his cunning against him. However, Coyote can not be destroyed. He has amazing powers of resurrection. Nowhere is this more clearly depicted than in the popular Coyote-Roadrunner cartoons. Althought he is drowned, crushed or falls from great heights Wily E. Coyote comes back to plot another trick.

Why have coyote stories lasted so long? Although they are entertaining one of the purposes of the legends is to point up a moral. Coyote serves as a model of what to do and what not to do. In many of the stories his anti-social behavior results in misfortune. Coyote stories also provide a relief from serious and tense concerns. Listeners or readers are able to take a vicarious delight in Coyote's irreverent attitude toward authority.

Coyote has the power to draw us all, no matter what our ethnic background, into his magic circle. In his own way, he serves to reinforce our human identity.

How It Happened Stories

THE MEDICINE MAN
(Isleta)

There is a telling that, in the beginning, when the animals first came up from the darkness to live above the ground, Coyote was sent ahead by Thought Woman to carry a buckskin pouch far to the south.

"You must be very careful not to open the pouch," she told him, "or you will be punished."

For many days, Coyote ran southward with the pouch on his back. But the world was new, and there was nothing to eat along the way, so he grew very hungry. He wondered if there might be food in the pouch. At last, he took it from his back and untied the thongs. He looked inside and saw nothing but stars. Of course, as soon as the pouch was opened, the stars all flew up into the sky, and there they are to this day.

"Now look what you've done," said Thought Woman. "For now you shall always get into trouble everywhere you go."

And because Coyote disobeyed, he was also made to suffer with the toothache. When the other animals were asleep, he could only sit and howl at the stars. Thus, he has been crying ever since the beginning of the world.

Sometimes he would ask the other animals to cure him, but they would only catch the toothache from him, and they, too, would cry.

One day, he met Mouse, who lived in a little mound under the chaparral bush. "Friend Mouse," begged Coyote, "can you cure me of this toothache?"

Now it happened that while digging underground, as is his habit, Mouse had come upon a sweet-smelling root and had put it with the other herbs in the pouch he always carried. He was said to be very wise in the use of herbs.

"I don't know," said Mouse, "but I have just found a new root, and it may be that it will help you." He rubbed the root on Coyote's swollen cheek, and in a little while the toothache was gone.

This is how it happened that coyotes never hunt or kill field mice.

THE STOLEN SQUASHES
(Acoma)

There is a telling that one day Insect Man went out to weed his squash patch and found that one of his squashes had been eaten.

"Who can the thief be?" he chirped. "I'll think of a way to catch him." So he sat down and thought for a while.

Then he took a sharp stick and went from one squash to another, tasting them all until he found the sweetest one in the whole patch. He chewed a small hole in it and crawled inside. "Now I shall find out who is stealing my squashes," he said.

Soon Coyote came trotting along. He stopped beside the patch and began tasting each squash. When he came to the sweet one, he ate it up, Insect Man and all.

Down inside Coyote, Insect Man hunted about, singing as usual. Coyote looked first on one side and then on the other. He could not see anyone and was puzzled about that singing.

At last, Insect Man found what he was looking for. He pushed his sharp stick as deep as he could into Coyote's heart, and Coyote fell over dead.

Insect Man crawled out and went back to his weeding and singing.

When Coyote came to life again, he never stole another squash. But that is how it happened that Coyotes have false hearts.

THE BROWN STONE EYES
(Zuni)

There is a telling about the crows that lived in the cedar canyon where Coyote had a habit of wandering to see what he could see. One day, he came near a wide, sandy place, and there were three crows amusing themselves by rolling their eyes on the ground.

Coyote sat back on his haunches, twitched his whiskers, and watched for awhile. Finally, being very curious, he asked, "Crow friends, what are you doing?"

"We are playing with our eyes," said the crows. "The one who rolls his eyes farthest wins the game."

"That is very nice," said Coyote. "I would like to play with you."

"Just as you like," said the crows. And they sent their eyes rolling down a little slope. "See if you can roll your eyes that far."

Coyote took out his eyes and rolled them as far as he could. But they did not go half as far as the crows' eyes had gone. The crows all laughed at Coyote.

"Let us try again," he growled, a little angered. "I'll beat you this time."

"Very well," agreed the crows, "but it is your turn first."

So Coyote tossed his eyes again. Now the crows knew what a fine meal they would make for Coyote if they were not careful. This time, as the eyes rolled along, they pounced on them and swallowed them. Then they flew away, laughing.

Coyote felt all around for his nice black eyes, but he could not find them. He would step on a small stone and cry, "Here they are." But each time he was mistaken. At last, he picked up two smooth pebbles. They were brown. "If I can't find my own eyes," he said, "I will have to use these stones for eyes."

He placed them in the sockets where his eyes had been. And that is how it happened that coyotes have brown eyes.

FIRE STORIES

THE SPOTTED DEER
(Jémez)

There is a telling about Coyote's meddlesome ways. One day, Deer Woman and her fawns were out gathering wood. Coyote sat beside the trail and watched while they tied the wood in bundles. Then he said, "Friend Deer Woman, how is it that your children are so prettily spotted?"

"Oh, that is from sitting around the fire," said Deer Woman. "When it burns, this cedar shoots out little sparks that light on their backs and make those spots."

So Coyote gathered a bundle of cedar and took it home on his back. That night, he built a big fire and told his children to sit close in a circle. The sparks began to jump from the fire and fall on the young coyotes' backs.

"The fire burns us," they whimpered.

"Sit still," scolded Coyote, "if you want to have pretty spots like the fawns."

But the longer they sat, the more the sparks burned, until their crying was too much even for Coyote to listen to.

And that is how it happened that the coyote's coat looks singed to this very day.

THE FALSE COLORS
(Taos)

There is a telling about the time Coyote tried to impress his neighbors, the Woodpecker family. Old Woodpecker lived in a hollow tree with his wife and children. One day, as Coyote ambled through the sagebrush, beneath the tree he met Old Woodpecker.

"How are you, friend Woodpecker?" he inquired politely.

"Very well, thank you. And how are you?" returned Old Woodpecker.

They talked together a while, and when they were about to part, Coyote said, "Friend Woodpecker, why do you not come to visit us? Come to our house for supper this evening, and bring your family."

"Thank you, friend Coyote," said Old Woodpecker. "We will come with pleasure."

So that evening, when Coyote Woman had supper ready, there came Old Woodpecker and his wife and children. Upon entering, the woodpeckers stretched themselves as is their habit on alighting, and thereby showed the pretty red and yellow feathers in their wings. During supper, too, they spread their wings and displayed the bright undersides.

The woodpeckers praised the fine supper made by Coyote Woman, and when it was time to leave, they thanked the coyotes and invited them to supper at their house the following evening.

Now Coyote, being naturally envious, brooded for some time after they were gone. "Did you notice the airs of those woodpeckers?" he said to his wife. "Always showing off their bright feathers."

Next day, Coyote put his family to work bringing in wood. Then he built a great fire. When it was time to visit the woodpeckers, he called his wife and children to the fire and fastened a burning stick under each of their arms.

"There," he said, "lift your arms now and then. You see, we are as handsome as the woodpeckers."

So they went to the house of the woodpeckers, lifting their arms often to show the bright coals underneath.

But as they sat down to supper, one of the young coyotes cried, "Oh, the fire is burning me!"

"Be patient," Coyote said severely, "and do not cry about little things."

"Oh," wept another young coyote, "my fire has gone out."

This was more than Coyote could stand, and he reproved her angrily.

"How is it, friend Coyote," asked Old Woodpecker, "that your colors are so bright at first but soon become dark?"

"That is the beauty of our colors," replied Coyote. "They are not always the same."

But the coyotes grew more uncomfortable and finally made an excuse to leave.

When they had gone, Old Woodpecker laughed and said to his children, 'Now you see why you should never try to appear other than you really are. Coyote always wants to be like others, but he never can. He is still Coyote."

And that is how it happened that his vanity brought them all to shame.

RACE STORIES

THE TAIL RACE
(Isleta)

There is a telling that once Coyote came where Rabbit sat by the entrance of his house. Rabbit was thinking.

"What are you thinking about, friend Rabbit?" asked Coyote.

"I am thinking, friend Coyote, why it must be that some animals have large tails like you, while we rabbits have scarcely any tail at all. Perhaps if we had tails like yours, we could run straight and not hop this way and that."

"It is true," said Coyote, very much flattered, "that I am a fleet runner, while you just hop like a bird."

"All the same," said Rabbit, "foot races are fun. Let us run a race around the world and see who will win."

"Very well," said Coyote. "In four days, we shall run. And whoever comes in first may kill and eat the other."

Then Rabbit went to visit his brothers and told them about the race. "We will think of a way to help you win," they said.

When the fourth day came, Coyote arrived and threw down his blanket. "But what is the use to run," he said, "for I shall win, anyway. It is better that I eat you now before you are tired."

Rabbit threw off his blanket and tightened his breechcloth, saying, "The end of the race is far away. Then it will be time enough to talk of eating. Come, we will run around the four sides of the world. I shall run underground because it is easier for me."

"It is all agreed, then," said Coyote. And when they were ready, they stood side by side. With a great shout, they started. Coyote ran with all his legs, and Rabbit jumped into a hole and began digging very fast, throwing out sand behind him.

For days, Coyote kept running to the east and saw nothing of Rabbit. But just as he came to the east and was turning north, up jumped Rabbit from under the ground in front of him. "We do this to one another," he hailed Coyote, and jumped back into the hole, throwing out dirt very hard.

I wish I could run underground, thought Coyote. *Surely it is easier, for I have run very fast all these days, and yet Rabbit came here ahead of me.* He could not know that Rabbit's brother had come out to the east to wait there.

So Coyote ran harder, and after many days, he came to the north and was about to turn west when Rabbit sprang up in front of him. "We do this to one another," he taunted, and jumped back into his hole, digging again.

Coyote's heart grew heavy, but he ran even harder than before. When he came to the west, Rabbit sprang up ahead of him as before. And when he ran to the south, it was the same again. At last, he came in sight of the starting point, and there was Rabbit sitting by the entrance of his house.

"Perhaps big tails are not better to run with, after all," said Rabbit, "since I have been waiting some time for you. Come here, Coyote, that I may eat you, though you are probably very tough."

But Coyote ran away and would not pay his debt.

Then Rabbit and his brothers laughed for the trick they had played on Coyote.

That is how it happened that his bragging ended in disgrace.

SONG STORIES

THE FORGOTTEN SONG
(Zuni)

There is a telling that one day Coyote was very hungry and decided he would try to catch some doves. He trotted toward the thicket where they lived, wondering how he might trick them.

On the way, he passed a large cottonwood tree where Woodpecker was singing.

"Good morning, Woodpecker Man," called Coyote. "You seem very happy today."

"Yes, I am," replied Woodpecker, "but you look sad. What troubles you, Coyote?"

"I am sad," said Coyote, "because I am so fond of the Dove People, and they do not like me."

"That is too bad," said Woodpecker sympathetically, and returned to his singing. When he looked down again, Coyote was still watching him.

"Perhaps," said Coyote, "if you would teach me your song, the Dove People would enjoy my company."

"Very well," said Woodpecker. So he sang the song over and over until Coyote could sing it, too.

When Coyote had gone off singing, Woodpecker said to himself, "That Coyote is sure to come back here bothering me again. He may not be so friendly the next time he comes."

So Woodpecker found a short tough stick and burned the end of it until it was glowing red. Then he flew up into the tree with it and stuck the other end into the hole he had been making in the tree trunk.

In the meantime, Coyote came to the thicket, but the Dove People were out in the tall grass eating seeds. They heard Coyote's strange voice singing, and it sounded so funny, they all flew up to see who it could be.

Coyote was taken by surprise and promptly forgot the song. Every time he tried to sing it, the Dove People laughed more and more, so Coyote hurried back to Woodpecker to learn the song again.

"I have forgotten your song, Woodpecker Man," he called up into the tree. "Will you please teach it to me again?"

There was no answer.

"I say, Woodpecker Man," called Coyote, growing impatient, "I have forgotten your song. Please teach it to me again."

Still there was no answer.

Coyote became angry. "If you do not sing it for me," he growled, "I will eat you up."

When there was still no answer, Coyote made a great leap and snapped at the charred stick with his teeth. The stick was still hot, and before he could drop it, his nose and whiskers were scorched.

That is how it happened that coyotes have black noses and whiskers even to this day.

THE THUNDER KNIVES
(Laguna)

There is a telling that one afternoon Old Coyote went out for a walk because it was that time of year when his grandchildren were so peevish that he could not sleep at home.

He came to a place on the sunny side of a big sandstone rock where Horned Toad was making pottery. As she moved the molding stone over the soft clay jar, she sang a song.

Old Coyote moved closer and listened. *That would be a fine song to soothe those young ones to sleep,* he thought.

But when Old Coyote came around the point of the rock, and Horned Toad saw him, she stopped singing.

"Friend Horned Toad," said Old Coyote, "please teach me that song so I can sing it to my grandchildren."

Horned Toad did not answer.

"Horned Toad," he repeated, "will you teach me that song you were singing?"

Still she did not answer.

"Horned Toad," said Old Coyote, losing his patience," if you do not teach me that song, I will eat you up."

At that, Horned Toad began to sing. And Old Coyote sang with her until he learned the song. "Now I must be going," he said, and trotted away singing the song.

About halfway home, he came to a small pond. There a flock of ducks suddenly flew up in front of him and caused him to spill the song. He looked about, turning over the stones and peering in the grass, but could not find the song.

Finally, he went back to ask Horned toad to teach

him the song again. "I was startled and spilled the song," he said to her. But there was no answer.

"Horned Toad," warned Old Coyote, "I will ask you four times, and if you do not teach me the song again, I will eat you up."

Still she did not reply. After asking four times, Old Coyote was enraged, so he swallowed the horned toad and started homeward.

When he was about halfway home, Old Coyote stopped and struck himself. "What a fool I am," he cried. "Now I am going home without the song. If I had just bothered Horned Toad long enough, she might have taught me the song again. I wish I could take her out and see if she would sing it for me . . ."

At that moment, Horned Toad lifted her thunder-knife spines and cut her way out. But Old Coyote fell over dead. So that is how it happened that he did not learn the pottery-making song.

THE JOLLY SNOWBIRDS
(Santo Domingo)

There is a telling that one bright morning the five Snowbird sisters were grinding acorns to make bread. As they ground the meal finer and finer on their sloping stones, they sang.

Coyote came along and heard the song from up the hill. He pricked up his ears, thinking how he might join them. Then, breaking off a branch of berries growing nearby, he trotted forward and knocked at their entrance.

"Come in," called the snowbirds cheerfully.

So Coyote stepped inside. "Good morning," he said. "How merry you are. Please let me grind with you."

When the snowbirds saw Coyote, they fluttered into a corner and left the grinding stones to him.

Coyote spread his berries over a stone and tried to grind and sing like the snowbirds. But the berries rolled about, and his song sounded so funny that the snowbirds forgot their fear and began to laugh.

The more Coyote tried to grind and sing, the funnier he looked, and the snowbirds laughed so hard that finally he tucked his tail between his legs and ran away.

And that is how it happened that pretending to be what he was not only got him laughed at.

THE PRAIRIE DOGS DANCE
(Cochiti)

There is a telling that on the mesa Coyote Grandfather lived. He had a little drum, and he used to sit above the road and beat the drum, singing:

> "Look out! Look out!
> Coyote is going to hit you
> On the back, on the back."

Whenever the prairie dogs heard this, they came running. "How beautifully you sing," they teased, and stepped in time to the song.

"Sing again," they pleaded when the old coyote paused to rest.

"Sing again, Coyote Grandfather. It is such fun to dance to your song."

One day, Skunk ran to the prairie-dog village. Old Coyote was dead, he told the little dogs. They must come and see. The prairie dogs thought this was good news if it were true, and they ran out to see for themselves.

There lay old Coyote stiff upon the ground.

"Let us dance and sing because he is dead and cannot bother us any more," they said.

So they began to dance around Old Coyote and to sing:

> "Look out! Look out!
> Coyote is going to hit you
> On the back, on the back."

Suddenly Old Coyote jumped up and began to strike the prairie dogs down. As he hit each one, Skunk caught it. When there were no more prairie dogs to taunt him, Old Coyote sat back, thinking what a fine meal he would have. But Skunk was nowhere to be seen, and he had made off with all the dogs. That is how it happened that Old Coyote outwitted himself.

TRICKSTER STORIES

THE PLAYFUL FAWNS
(Jémez)

There is a telling about Coyote's habit of wanting everything he saw. One morning, he was traveling just above the canyon and heard some fawns singing. He crouched in the brush to listen and then crept close enough to see what was going on.

In the warm sand between the cedars, the Fawn Children were playing. Coyote ambled out of hiding and spoke to them.

"Good morning, Fawn Children. You sound very happy today. What is that game you are playing?"

"Oh, we were admiring our new antlers."

Now Coyote had always envied the beautiful antlers worn by the deer, so he said, "Please tell me where you got them."

"They were fastened to our heads by our mother. It is very simple."

"Do you think that if I found some antlers, they could be fastened to my head?" asked Coyote hopefully.

"We will gladly do it for you," said the fawns. And they began to sing again.

Coyote hurried off. But he was soon back with a pair of large antlers. He put his head down for the fawns to fasten them on.

"Of course, we are much younger than you," they said. "This may hurt your tough old head a little."

"But think how handsome I shall be," said Coyote.

"Very well, then, hold still." So the fawns took a large stone and drove the antlers into Coyote's head.

He howled with pain while the fawns ran away, laughing. That is how it happened that deer and coyotes are no longer friends.

THE TURKEY'S MESSAGE
(San Juan)

There is a telling about Coyote's habit of laziness. A little snow had fallen in the night, so Coyote said to his wife, "I had better go out hunting."

He went up the hill to the top of the mesa. There he met Old Turkey.

"What luck," he said to himself. "I am not yet tired, and here I find a turkey." He told Old Turkey to go to his house and tell his wife to make some turkey stew.

"But how shall I find your house that your wife may cook me?" asked Old Turkey.

"You can follow my tracks in the snow," said Coyote. "I will go on hunting."

After Old Turkey had gone, Coyote said to himself, "There is no need to hunt anymore. I will sleep a while in the sun."

When Old Turkey came to where Coyote lived, he said to Coyote Woman, "I met your husband on the mesa, and he told me you had hanging up some sinew that you should take down and cook for supper."

"I wonder why he wants me to cook that. What will he make moccasins with? Well, Old Turkey has brought me that message. I had better cook it."

Then Old Turkey flew away to his range.

Coyote slept soundly in the sunshine all day. In the evening, he got up. "I am very hungry," he said, "but I shall have a good supper." So he went straight to his house. He saw the turkey tracks up to the entrance.

His wife put out the stew, and he began to eat. "this turkey is as tough as sinew," he complained.

"Old Turkey came here today," said is wife. "He told

47

me you wanted that sinew cooked for supper."

"That Old Turkey cheated me," grumbled Coyote.

And that is how it happened that living on expectation led him only to disappointment.

The World Catches Fire
(Taos)

There is a telling about Flycatcher, who lived on the dry prairie. She had her nest on the ground. Coyote was out hunting as usual and saw the young birds in the nest. He stopped and looked at them. "What are you doing?" he asked.

"Nothing," they replied.

"You look nice and fat. Where is your mother?"

Now Flycatcher had told them that if Coyote should come along, they were to open their mouths wide so as to scare him away. So they opened their mouths as wide as they could.

Coyote ran off to his house in a great fright. Before entering, he looked back and saw the spot where the nest was and the birds with their mouths still wide open and red as fire.

"The world is on fire," he shouted from his roof top to all the other animals. To his family, he cried, "Come, we must go to the river where we shall be safe."

When they arrived, he made all his family jump into the water. They swam around until they became tired and drowned.

The other animals waited, but nothing could be seen of the burning world. So they decided to see where Coyote and his family had gone. They followed the footprints to the river.

Then they said, "Because Coyote is so cowardly, he always finds trouble before it can find him. That is how Thought Woman said it would be." And that is how it all happened.

THE DISCONTENTED FARMER
(Isleta)

There is a telling that one time Coyote was going about as he always does and chanced to meet Bear by the river. They talked for a while, and then Bear said, "Friend Coyote, do you see this good land? What do you say we farm it together and share the crop?"

Coyote thought well of this and said so.

They agreed to plant potatoes.

"I have thought of a good way to divide the crop," said Bear. "I will take all that grows below the ground, and you take all that grows above it. Each can take his share when he is ready, and there will be no bother of measuring."

"Very well," said Coyote. So together they worked the earth with a sharp stick and planted the potatoes. All summer they cut out the weeds and let in water from the irrigation ditch.

When harvest time came, Coyote gathered all the potato tops and carried them home. Bear dug the roots out of the ground with his strong claws and took them to his house.

A little time later, Coyote met Bear and said, "That crop division was not fair. You have all those roots, which are good to eat. The tops I took home, neither my wife nor I can eat at all."

"But, friend Coyote," said Bear, "that was our agreement."

So Coyote went home, but he was not satisfied.

Next spring, they met again, and Bear said, "Come, friend Coyote, I think we should plant this good land again. Last year, you were dissatisfied with your share, so this year we will change about. You take what is below ground, and I will take only what grows above it."

This seemed fair to Coyote, so he agreed.

They decided this time to plant corn. All summer they tended the field, and when it came harvest time, Bear gathered the stalks and ears and carried them home.

When Coyote came to dig his roots, he found they were not fat and tasty like those of the previous year but thin and good for nothing. He complained to Bear, who only reminded him again of his bargain.

And that is how it happened that wisdom came to the foolish Coyote — too late.

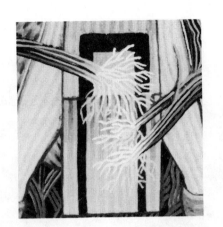

THE PINE GUM BABY
(Santa Clara)

There is a telling that one spring Coyote decided to grow some melons. He planted the seeds and tended the young vines, and whenever he was not out hunting, he was working in his melon patch.

One morning, when the fat melons were almost ready to gather, he found that two of them had been stolen. Coyote growled and looked all around the patch but could find not a single track because the vines were so thick they covered the ground.

Next morning, two more melons were gone. This time, Coyote searched harder than before, and at last he found some scratches where someone had squeezed under the fence.

"Ah, here is where the thief came in," he cried. "I'll fix him, that Rabbit Boy."

So he trotted off to a large pinyon tree and gathered a jar full of pine gum. He shaped the gum into a baby and set it near the hole under the fence.

That night, Rabbit came quietly in the moonlight as he had before. But when he crawled through the hole and saw the gum baby sitting in his way, he was a little annoyed.

"Good evening," he said, pretending politeness. "Will you be so kind as to let me pass?"

But the gum baby neither answered his greeting nor moved aside.

"Good evening, I say, will you let me pass?"

Still gum baby did not move. Rabbit was more annoyed than ever. He lifted his paw and gave the gum baby a shove, but his paw stuck fast.

"Turn me loose," shouted Rabbit as he pulled and tugged to get away. "Turn me loose, or I'll hit you again."

But the gum baby held him fast. So Rabbit hit him as hard as he could with the other paw. It stuck as fast as the first.

"Maybe you think I can't kick you," he cried. "You had better turn me loose before I kick you." And Rabbit hauled off and kicked as hard as he could. There was his foot, stuck fast. This made him so angry that he kicked fiercely with his other foot, and then it was stuck, too.

"I will butt you," raged Rabbit, butting the gum baby with his head. And it stuck, too. So there he was, stuck fast to that gum baby. He rolled and struggled to get loose but only stuck faster than ever.

When the sun came up, Coyote ran out to see if he had caught Rabbit. "So, I have caught you at last Rabbit Boy. Now I shall eat you for stealing my melons."

"I was only passing by," said Rabbit. "And this gum baby was so rude I had to hit him. Please take me off."

"I will eat you off," said Coyote.

"Well, I would not taste very good," said Rabbit. "I am all sticky."

"I guess that's right," said Coyote. "I'll have to take you down by the river and wash you off."

And so he did.

"Now I shall have a good meal," said Coyote.

'But please don't eat me here," begged Rabbit. "The rains would carry my bones away and scatter them so that I could never come to life again. Then you would have no more rabbit to eat."

"Where can I eat you, then?" asked Coyote.

"Put me down for a minute so I can think," said Rabbit.

When Coyote put him down, Rabbit bounded away beyond Coyote's reach.

That is how it happened that the trick was turned upon himself.

BIBLIOGRAPHY

Barclay, Lillian
"The Coyote: Animal and Folk Character."
Texas Folklore Society Publications
Vol. 14 (1938) pp. 36-103.

Benedict, Ruth
Tales of the Cochiti Indians.
Albuquerque: University of New Mexico
    Press, 1981.

Bernstein, Margery
Coyote Goes Hunting for Fire: a California Indian Myth.
New York: Scribner, 1974.

Blue Cloud, Peter
Elderberry Flute Song: Contemporary Coyote Tales.
Trumansburg, NY: Crossing Press, 1982.

Bonnin, Gertrude
Old Indian Legends.
Lincoln: University of Nebraska Press, 1985.

Bright, William, Ed.
Coyote Stories.
Chicago: University of Chicago Press, 1978.

Canonge, Elliott
Comanche Texts.
Norman: Summer Institute of Linguistics of the
    University of Oklahoma, 1958.

Carlisle, Veronica M.
"Notes on the Coyote in Southwestern
    Folktales."
Affword Vol.3, No.4 (Winter 1973) pp.38-47.

Courlander, Harold
People of the Short Blue Corn.
New York: Harcourt Brace Jovanovich, 1970.

Coyote's Journal
Berkeley, CA: Wingbow, 1982.

Dobie, J. Frank
"Coyote: Hero-God and Trickster."
Southwest Review Vol.32 (1947) pp.336-344.

————————.
"Coyote Wisdom"
Austin: Texas Folklore Society Publications.
    Vol.14 (1938)

————————.
The Voice of the Coyote.
Boston: Little, Brown, 1949.

Dutton, Bertha P.
Indians of the American Southwest.
Englewood Cliffs, NJ: Prentice-Hall, 1975.

Haile, Berard
Navajo Coyote Tales, the Curly To'Aheedliinii Version.
Lincoln: University of Nebraska Press, 1984.
    (American Tribal Religious, vol.8)

Hayes, Joe
Coyote And: Native American Folk Tales.
Santa Fe, NM: Mariposa, 1983.

Jones, Hettie
Coyote Tales.
New York: Holt, 1974.

Leydet, Francois
The Coyote: Defiant Songdog of the West.
Norman: University of Oklahoma Press, 1979.

Linderman, Frank Bird
Old Man Coyote.
New York: John Day, 1931.

Lopez, Barry Holstun
Giving Birth to Thunder, Sleeping With His Daughter.
    Coyote Builds North America.
Kansas City: Sheed Andrews and McMeel, 1978.

Lummis, Charles Fletcher
Pueblo Indian Folk-Stories.
New York: Century, 1910.

Malotki, Ekkehart
Gullible Coyote. Una'ihu. A Bilingual Collection of
    Hopi Coyote Stories.
Tucson: University of Arizona Press, 1985.

Malotki, Ekkehart and Lomatuway'ma, Michael
Hopi Coyote Tales (Istutuwutsi)
Lincoln: University of Nebraska Press, 1984.
(American Tribal Religions, Vol.9)

Milford, Stanley J.
"Why the Coyote Has a Black Spot On His Tail."
Santa Fe, NM: El Palacio. Vol.48, No.4 (1941)
    pp.83-84.

Monroe, Jean Guard and Williamson, Ray A.
They Dance in the Sky
Boston: Houghton Mifflin, 1987.

Morgan, William
Coyote Tales.
Washington, DC: U.S. Bureau of Indian
    Affairs, 1954.
Navajo and English text.
(Navajo Life Series)

Mourning Dove |Mowrning Dore (Humishuma)|
Coyote Stories.
Caldwell, ID: Caxton, 1953.

——————————.
——————————.
New York: AMS Press, 1976

Opler, Morris Edward
Myths and Tales of the Chiricahua Apache Indians.
Memoirs of the American Folklore Society,
    No.37 (1942)

——————————.
Myths and Tales of the Jicarilla Apache Indians.
Memoirs of the American Folklore Society,
    No.31 (1938)

——————————.
Myths and Legends of the Lipan Apache Indians.
Memoirs of the American Folklore Society,
    No.36 (1940)

Otis, Alicia
Spiderwoman's Dream.
Santa Fe, NM: Sunstone Press, 1987.

Palmer, William R.
Pahute Indian Legends.
Salt Lake City, UT: Deseret Book Co., 1946.

Pletcher, D.E.
"Coyote Scatters the Stars;
    Cochiti Pueblo Indian Myth."
Nature Magazine. 24.280 (Dec., 1934)

Pringle, Laurence
The Controversial Coyote.
New York: Harcourt, Brace, 1977.

Radin, Paul
The Trickster.
New York: Schocken, 1972.

Ramsey, Jarold
*Coyote Was Going There: Indian Literature of
    the Oregon Country.*
Seattle: University of Washington Press, 1977.

Reichard, Gladys A.
An Analysis of Coeur' d'Alene Indian Myths.
Philadelphia, PA: American Folklore Society, 1947.

Roessel, Robert A., Jr. and Roessel, Dillon
Coyote Stories of the Navajo People.
Phoenix, AZ: Navajo Curriculum Center
    Press, 1968.

Rothenberg, Jerome
*Shaking the Pumpkin. Traditional Poetry of
    the Indian North Americas.*
New York: Alfred Van Der Marck Editions, 1986.
Revised edition.

Ryden, Hope
God's Dog.
New York: Viking, 1979.

Simpson, Ruth DeEtte
"The Coyote in Southwestern Indian Tradition."
The Masterkey. 32:2 (March-April, 1958)

Snyder, Gary
The Old Ways.
San Francisco, CA: City Lights Books, 1977.

Thompson, Stith
Tales of the North American Indians.
Bloomington, IN: Indiana University Press, 1966.

VanEtten, Teresa
Ways of Indian Wisdom.
Santa Fe, NM: Sunstone Press, 1987.

Williamson, Ray A.
Living the Sky. The Cosmos of the American Indian.
Boston, MA: Houghton, Mifflin, 1984.

Young, Stanley P. and Jackson, Hartley H.
The Clever Coyote.
Lincoln: University of Nebraska Press, 1978.

Send for our free catalog

and find out more about our books on:

- ❖ The Old West
- ❖ American Indian subjects
- ❖ Western Fiction
- ❖ Architecture
- ❖ Hispanic interest subjects
- ❖ And our line of full-color notecards

Just mail this card or call us on our toll-free number below

Name

Address

City   State   Zip

Send Book Catalog _____   Send Notecard Catalog _____

Sunstone Press / P.O.Box 2321 / Santa Fe, NM 87504
(505) 988-4418   FAX (505) 988-1025   (800)-243-5644